RICHARD M.A. RUSSELL

Subversion- The Hidden War

Defending Democracy in the Age of Information Warfare

Contents

Introduction: The New Face of War … 1

Chapter 1: Demoralization - The Foundation of Subversion … 3
What is Demoralization? … 3
Education: Shaping Minds for the Future … 4
Religion: Undermining the Moral Bedrock … 5
Media and Culture: The Erosion of Trust … 6
Social Life and Relationships: The Breakdown of Community … 7

Chapter 2: Destabilization - When Society Teeters … 9
What is Destabilization? … 9
The Economy: Shaking the Pillars of Prosperity … 10
Law and Order: Eroding Public Trust … 11
Political Polarization: Driving the Wedge Deeper … 12
Cultural Radicalization: Exploiting Identity and Beliefs … 14
Conclusion of Chapter 2: … 15

Chapter 3: Crisis - The Point of No Return … 16
What is Crisis? … 16
Institutional Breakdown: When Systems Fail … 17
Widespread Panic: The Loss of Public Confidence … 18
Radical Responses: The Lure of Extremism … 19
Manufactured Crises: When Crisis is a Strategy … 21
Crisis and Opportunity: The Thin Line Between
Collapse and Transformation … 22
Conclusion of Chapter 3: … 23

Chapter 4: Normalization - The Final Stage … 24
What is Normalization? … 24

Consolidation of Power: Cementing the New Order   25

Suppression of Opposition: Silencing Dissent   27

Rewriting of History: Controlling the Narrative   28

Institutional Reconfiguration: Reshaping Society   29

Normalization and Its Consequences: Stability at a Price   30

Conclusion of Chapter 4:   31

Chapter 5: The Subversion of Western Democracies   33

The Role of Social Media: A Tool for Domestic Subversion   34

The Crisis of Identity Politics: Fragmenting Societies   35

Foreign Influence: A Global Game of Subversion   37

Conclusion of Chapter 5:   38

Chapter 6: The New Cold War - Subversion in the
Age of...   40

Russia's Playbook: Hybrid Warfare and Strategic Influence   41

China's Silent Influence: Economic Power and
Strategic Subversion   43

The West's Role: A Complex History of Influence Operations   45

The Role of Cyber Warfare: A New Battlefield   46

Conclusion of Chapter 6:   48

Chapter 7: The Future of Subversion - Emerging
Threats in...   49

Artificial Intelligence and Disinformation: The
Next Frontier   50

Weaponization of Globalization: Economic Lever-
age and Strategic Dependency   52

The Interconnectedness of Global Systems: New
Vulnerabilities and Opportunities   54

Conclusion of Chapter 7:   55

Resilience and Counter-Subversion - Strategies for a Secure...   57

Chapter 8: Strengthening Democratic Resilience   58

Fortifying Democratic Institutions   58

Encouraging Civic Engagement   59
Maintaining Transparency and Accountability   60
Building Cybersecurity Alliances   61
Strengthening Multilateral Institutions   62
Chapter 10: The Role of Technology and Innovation   64
Harnessing Artificial Intelligence for Good   64
Balancing Innovation with Ethics   65
Chapter 11: Education, Media Literacy, and Public Awareness   66
Promoting Media Literacy   66
Fostering a Culture of Critical Thinking   67
Building Trust Through Transparency   67
Conclusion: A Blueprint for Resilience   68

Introduction: The New Face of War

War isn't always fought with guns and bombs. In the 21st century, a more insidious form of conflict is taking place—a battle that happens in classrooms, media outlets, and even in our own minds. This war is one of ideas, values, and perceptions, and its name is subversion.

Subversion isn't about dramatic explosions or secret agents in trench coats. It's a silent siege, a slow and steady process of undermining a society's foundations from within. It doesn't aim to destroy buildings or infrastructure directly but seeks to erode the moral, cultural, and political structures that hold a nation together. The goal? To weaken a society to the point where it collapses or becomes so destabilized that it can be easily taken over, often without a single shot being fired.

In this book, we'll explore how subversion works, how it's been used throughout history, and how it continues to shape the world today. We'll look at real-world examples, from the Soviet Union's Cold War tactics to the subtle influences of modern-day information warfare. Most importantly, we'll discuss what can be done to resist this form of warfare, safeguarding the values and freedoms that are often its primary targets.

This book isn't about creating paranoia or assigning blame. Instead, it's about awareness—understanding the subtle ways in which our perceptions can be manipulated and how we can build resilience against such threats. Whether you're a student, a teacher, a professional, or just someone curious about how the world really works, this book is for you.

So, let's dive into the world of subversion—a battlefield where the fight for the future isn't fought with weapons, but with ideas.

Chapter 1: Demoralization - The Foundation of Subversion

Imagine a society where people no longer trust their leaders, where institutions that once commanded respect are now met with skepticism or outright disdain. Where once-unifying values are dismissed as outdated or irrelevant, and the fabric of community life is frayed by individualism and division. This is the world that demoralization creates.

What is Demoralization?

Demoralization is the first stage of subversion, and it's the most fundamental. It's a process that takes years, even decades, to unfold— usually 15 to 20 years, the time it takes to raise and educate a new generation. During this time, the goal is to gradually erode the moral and intellectual foundations of a society, making it more vulnerable to influence and control from external or subversive forces.

But how exactly does this happen? Demoralization isn't about a single event or policy change. It's about subtle, cumulative shifts in culture, education, religion, media, and social life that together create a society ripe for destabilization. Let's break down the key areas targeted during this stage.

Education: Shaping Minds for the Future

The classroom is where the future of any society is forged. It's where young minds are shaped, where they learn not just facts and figures, but also values, critical thinking, and a sense of identity. Demoralization often starts here, subtly altering what and how students are taught.

Case Study: The Changing Focus of Education in America

Over the past few decades, there has been a noticeable shift in American education. Once, the focus was on subjects like mathematics, science, and history—fields that are concrete, fact-based, and essential for understanding the world and contributing to society. But increasingly, there has been a move toward more subjective areas of study, such as social justice, gender studies, and postmodern theory.

While these subjects have their place, the concern arises when they begin to overshadow core disciplines, leading to a generation less equipped to think critically or engage with the complexities of the world. This isn't about one ideology being better than another—it's about ensuring that education remains balanced, providing students with the tools they need to navigate life, rather than indoctrinating them with a particular worldview.

The impact? Students may graduate with strong opinions but lack the practical skills needed in the workforce or the critical thinking abilities required to engage with different perspectives. This shift contributes to a broader societal divide, where people are more likely to see those who disagree with them not just as wrong, but as morally inferior.

Analysis: The Long-Term Consequences

When education becomes a tool for ideological subversion, its effects are long-lasting. A generation raised on a skewed understanding of their history, culture, and society is more likely to question the legitimacy of the very institutions that govern them. This paves the way for increasing polarization, where common ground is lost, and societal cohesion begins to crumble.

Religion: Undermining the Moral Bedrock

Religion has traditionally been a cornerstone of moral and ethical guidance in many societies. It offers not just a set of beliefs, but a framework for community, mutual respect, and shared values. Subversion targets religion by either eroding its influence or replacing it with something else entirely.

Case Study: The Decline of Traditional Religions in the West

In recent years, there has been a marked decline in religious adherence in Western countries. Churches that were once central to community life are now closing their doors, and religious teachings are increasingly viewed as outdated or irrelevant. In their place, we see the rise of secular ideologies and new spiritual movements, many of which prioritize individual fulfillment over communal values.

While the decline in traditional religion is often framed as a move toward progress and enlightenment, it also represents a weakening of the moral and ethical structures that have held societies together for centuries. When religion is replaced by ideologies that lack a deep moral framework, the result can be a society that is more fragmented, less cohesive, and more susceptible to manipulation.

Analysis: The Role of Religion in Social Stability

Religion, at its best, provides a shared set of values that transcend individual differences, helping to unite people around common principles. When these shared values are eroded, society becomes more vulnerable to division and conflict. This doesn't mean that everyone needs to adhere to the same religion, but it does suggest that a society without a strong moral framework is more likely to fall prey to subversive influences.

Media and Culture: The Erosion of Trust

The media is often referred to as the "fourth estate," a vital check on power and a source of information for the public. But what happens when the media itself becomes a tool of subversion?

Case Study: The Portrayal of Authority Figures in Modern Media

Over the past few decades, there has been a noticeable shift in how authority figures—such as police officers, military personnel, and even political leaders—are portrayed in popular media. In many films and television shows, these figures are depicted as corrupt, incompetent, or even malevolent. While it's important to hold power to account, this consistent portrayal can erode public trust in the very institutions that maintain social order.

This trend isn't limited to fictional media. News outlets, too, often focus on negative stories, giving disproportionate attention to scandals and failures while downplaying or ignoring positive developments. The result is a public that is increasingly cynical and distrustful, not just of individual leaders, but of the entire system.

Analysis: The Impact on Public Perception

When trust in authority is undermined, it becomes easier to push a narrative that the system itself is broken and in need of radical change. This opens the door to extremist ideologies and movements that promise to fix what is supposedly beyond repair. But often, these "solutions" are far worse than the problems they aim to address, leading to further destabilization.

Social Life and Relationships: The Breakdown of Community

At its core, subversion seeks to isolate individuals, making them more dependent on the state or other controlling entities. One of the ways this is achieved is by undermining the traditional social structures that provide support and a sense of belonging.

Case Study: The Rise of State-Dependent Social Programs

In many Western societies, there has been a significant increase in state-funded social programs, from welfare to social workers intervening in family life. While these programs often provide necessary support, they can also weaken the natural bonds between individuals and their communities. Where once people turned to family, neighbors, or religious groups for help, they now turn to the state.

This shift isn't inherently negative, but it can become problematic when it leads to a loss of personal responsibility and community engagement. When people rely on impersonal bureaucracies rather than personal connections, it's easier for those in power to manipulate them, using the promise of security to justify greater control.

Analysis: The Consequences of Dependency

As communities weaken and individuals become more isolated, society as a whole becomes easier to manipulate. When people no longer feel connected to those around them, they're more likely to accept narratives that emphasize division and conflict. This plays directly into the hands of those who seek to destabilize society from within.

Conclusion of Chapter 1:

Demoralization is a slow process, but its effects are profound. By targeting education, religion, media, and social life, subversive forces can weaken the very foundations of a society, making it vulnerable to further destabilization. The key to resisting this stage of subversion lies in awareness—recognizing the subtle shifts that are taking place and taking steps to reinforce the values and institutions that hold society together.

In the next chapter, we'll explore the second stage of subversion: destabilization. Here, we'll see how the groundwork laid during demoralization is exploited to push society to the brink of crisis.

Chapter 2: Destabilization - When Society Teeters

If demoralization is the slow erosion of a society's foundation, destabilization is the point where the cracks start to show. It's the phase where existing tensions, previously manageable, begin to spiral out of control. Destabilization doesn't need to rely on dramatic upheavals—though they often happen. Instead, it feeds on existing divisions, exacerbating conflicts to the point where compromise seems impossible, and society edges closer to crisis.

What is Destabilization?

Destabilization is the second stage of subversion. It targets the critical structures that keep a society functioning: the economy, law and order, and the political system. Unlike demoralization, which is a long-term process, destabilization can happen much more quickly. The aim is to push the society into a state of chaos where normal political processes are disrupted, and extremist solutions start to seem like the only way out.

Key Areas of Destabilization

1. **The Economy:** Undermining the financial stability of a nation.
2. **Law and Order:** Eroding the effectiveness of police, courts, and the legal system.
3. **Political Polarization:** Driving wedges between different political factions, making governance increasingly difficult.

Let's dive into each of these areas to see how destabilization plays out in practice.

The Economy: Shaking the Pillars of Prosperity

A stable economy is the backbone of any society. It provides the jobs, services, and resources that people need to live their lives and pursue their goals. Destabilization targets the economy to create uncertainty and fear, pushing people toward extreme measures.

Case Study: The Global Financial Crisis of 2008

The 2008 financial crisis was a seismic event that shook the global economy to its core. While it was caused by a complex mix of factors—irresponsible lending practices, speculative bubbles, and a lack of regulatory oversight—it also provides a textbook example of how economic destabilization can bring a society to the brink of collapse.

In the United States, millions lost their homes, jobs, and savings almost overnight. The ripple effects were felt worldwide, leading to widespread economic hardship and a deep sense of insecurity. Governments scrambled to respond, but the damage was done. Trust in financial institutions plummeted, and the crisis sparked political movements on both the left and right that would dramatically reshape the political landscape.

Analysis: How Economic Crisis Breeds Extremism

When the economy collapses, people naturally look for someone to blame. This is fertile ground for extremist ideologies, which promise simple solutions to complex problems. In the aftermath of the 2008 crisis, we saw the rise of movements like the Tea Party in the United States, which channeled public anger toward the government, and the Occupy Wall Street movement, which targeted the financial elite.

In Europe, the crisis fueled the rise of populist parties on both the left and the right, challenging the political status quo and deepening divisions within and between countries. These movements capitalized on economic uncertainty, pushing society further toward destabilization.

Law and Order: Eroding Public Trust

A society's laws and the institutions that enforce them are essential for maintaining order and protecting citizens' rights. Destabilization targets these institutions, weakening their ability to function effectively and undermining public trust.

Case Study: The Ferguson Protests and Their Aftermath

In 2014, the shooting of Michael Brown, an unarmed Black teenager, by a white police officer in Ferguson, Missouri, sparked a wave of protests across the United States. The incident highlighted longstanding tensions between police and minority communities, particularly regarding the use of force and racial profiling.

The protests quickly spread beyond Ferguson, leading to a national conversation about race, policing, and justice. While the protests brought much-needed attention to these issues, they also exposed deep divisions in American society. Some saw the police as protectors of public safety, while others viewed them as oppressors. The resulting polarization made it difficult to find common ground, and the trust between law enforcement and the communities they serve was severely damaged.

Analysis: The Dangers of Polarized Policing

When public trust in law enforcement erodes, the very fabric of society is threatened. If people no longer believe that the police will protect them—or worse, if they believe that the police are a danger—they are less likely to cooperate with law enforcement or follow the law themselves. This can lead to an increase in crime, vigilantism, and social unrest, further destabilizing society.

The Ferguson protests and their aftermath illustrate how quickly law and order can break down when trust is lost. It also shows how destabilization can feed on existing societal tensions, turning manageable conflicts into full-blown crises.

Political Polarization: Driving the Wedge Deeper

Political polarization is a key tool of destabilization. By turning politics into a zero-sum game where compromise is seen as betrayal, destabilizers can paralyze governments, making it impossible for them to address the needs of their citizens.

Case Study: The Rise of Hyper-Partisanship in the United States

In the past few decades, American politics has become increasingly polarized. The divide between Democrats and Republicans has grown wider, with both sides viewing each other not just as opponents, but as enemies. This hyper-partisanship has made it difficult for Congress to pass legislation, even on issues where there is broad public support.

The polarization has been fueled by a variety of factors, including the rise of partisan media, gerrymandering, and the influence of money in politics. But it has also been exacerbated by subversive forces, both foreign and domestic, that seek to widen the divide for their own gain.

Analysis: The Paralysis of Governance

When a political system becomes too polarized, it can no longer function effectively. Legislators become more focused on defeating their opponents than on governing, leading to gridlock and a failure to address pressing issues. This, in turn, fuels public frustration and disillusionment, making it easier for extremist movements to gain traction.

The rise of hyper-partisanship in the United States is a clear example of how destabilization can cripple a government's ability to function. It shows how political polarization can be both a cause and an effect of destabilization, creating a vicious cycle that is difficult to break.

Cultural Radicalization: Exploiting Identity and Beliefs

Another facet of destabilization is the radicalization of cultural identities. By amplifying differences and pitting groups against one another, destabilizers can fragment society along racial, religious, or ideological lines.

Case Study: The Cultural Divide Over Immigration in Europe

Immigration has been a contentious issue in Europe for decades, but it reached a boiling point during the refugee crisis of 2015. The arrival of millions of refugees from Syria, Afghanistan, and other conflict zones sparked intense debates across the continent about national identity, security, and the future of the European Union.

In many countries, the crisis fueled the rise of far-right parties that exploited fears of immigration to gain support. These parties framed immigration as an existential threat to European culture and values, leading to a sharp increase in xenophobia and anti-immigrant sentiment. At the same time, progressive groups rallied around the cause of refugee rights, leading to a deep cultural divide.

Analysis: The Perils of Identity Politics

When cultural identities are politicized, it becomes easier for destabilizers to create divisions within society. By framing issues like immigration in terms of "us versus them," they can rally support from those who feel threatened, while further alienating those who feel marginalized. This can lead to increased social tension, violence, and ultimately, a breakdown in the social fabric.

The cultural divide over immigration in Europe illustrates how destabilization can exploit identity politics to fragment society. It also shows how difficult it can be to heal these divisions once they have been opened.

Conclusion of Chapter 2:

Destabilization is a dangerous and volatile phase in the process of subversion. It targets the key structures that keep society functioning—economy, law and order, and political systems—turning manageable problems into full-blown crises. By exacerbating existing divisions and undermining trust in institutions, destabilization creates the conditions for further chaos and conflict.

The key to resisting destabilization lies in resilience—both of institutions and individuals. This means strengthening democratic processes, fostering social cohesion, and maintaining trust in the systems that govern society. It also means being aware of the ways in which subversive forces seek to exploit our differences and using that awareness to build bridges rather than walls.

In the next chapter, we'll explore the third stage of subversion: crisis. We'll see how the destabilization process reaches its climax, pushing societies to the brink of collapse and setting the stage for radical change.

Chapter 3: Crisis - The Point of No Return

Crisis is the tipping point. It's the moment when destabilization reaches critical mass, and society is thrown into a state of turmoil that threatens to tear it apart. Unlike demoralization and destabilization, which can unfold gradually, crisis often erupts suddenly. It's the stage where the cracks that were previously just visible widen into chasms, and where the very survival of the society, as it was known, is at stake.

In this chapter, we'll explore how crises are engineered or exacerbated by subversive forces, the various forms they can take, and the devastating impact they can have on nations. We'll also look at real-world examples of crises that have brought societies to their knees, examining the factors that pushed them over the edge and the aftermath that followed.

What is Crisis?

Crisis is the third stage of subversion, where society is pushed to the brink of collapse. It's a moment of intense danger and uncertainty, where the normal rules no longer seem to apply, and where radical solutions—often unthinkable just a short time before—start to gain traction.

A crisis can take many forms. It might be economic, like a stock market crash or a wave of bank failures. It could be political, like a coup or a contested election. It might be social, like widespread civil unrest or a breakdown in law and order. Or it could be a combination of all these factors, creating a perfect storm that overwhelms the system.

The Hallmarks of Crisis

1. **Institutional Breakdown:** Established institutions, whether governmental, economic, or social, cease to function effectively.
2. **Widespread Panic:** The public loses faith in the ability of existing structures to address the crisis, leading to fear, uncertainty, and often violence.
3. **Radical Responses:** In the face of chaos, extremist solutions become more attractive, paving the way for dramatic shifts in power.

Let's delve into how crises unfold and how subversive elements can manipulate them to achieve their goals.

Institutional Breakdown: When Systems Fail

The first sign of crisis is often the breakdown of the institutions that are supposed to hold society together. When these institutions fail—whether they are banks, courts, governments, or social services—the effects can be devastating.

Case Study: The Collapse of the Soviet Union

One of the most dramatic examples of institutional breakdown in recent history is the collapse of the Soviet Union in the early 1990s. For decades, the Soviet Union was one of the world's two superpowers, with a vast military, a controlled economy, and a government that maintained strict control over its people. But by the late 1980s, cracks were beginning to show.

Economic stagnation, political corruption, and growing public dissatisfaction weakened the Soviet system from within. Gorbachev's reforms, intended to revitalize the economy and increase political openness, instead accelerated the process of collapse. As the central government lost control, nationalist movements within the Soviet republics gained momentum, demanding independence.

The crisis came to a head in 1991 when a failed coup by hardline Communists further eroded the central government's authority. By the end of that year, the Soviet Union had dissolved, and its constituent republics became independent nations.

Analysis: How Institutional Breakdown Leads to Crisis

The collapse of the Soviet Union shows how quickly a seemingly stable system can unravel when its institutions fail. Once the public loses faith in these institutions, the entire structure of society can collapse, creating a power vacuum that is often filled by radical or opportunistic forces. This kind of institutional breakdown is a key indicator of crisis, and it's often the moment when a society is most vulnerable to subversive elements.

Widespread Panic: The Loss of Public Confidence

When institutions break down, the public's reaction is often one of panic. This is a natural response to uncertainty, but it can also be highly destabilizing. Panic can take many forms—economic, social, or political—and it often leads to rash decisions that exacerbate the crisis.

Case Study: The Great Depression

The Great Depression of the 1930s is one of the most famous examples of widespread panic contributing to a national crisis. The stock market crash of 1929 triggered a wave of bank failures, as panicked depositors rushed to withdraw their savings. As banks collapsed, credit dried up, businesses closed, and millions of people lost their jobs.

The Depression was not just an economic crisis; it was also a crisis of confidence. People lost faith in the financial system, in the government, and in the future. This sense of despair led to social unrest, as seen in the rise of extremist movements in Europe, and political instability, as democratic governments struggled to cope with the scale of the disaster.

Analysis: The Ripple Effect of Panic

Panic is contagious. Once it takes hold, it can spread rapidly through a society, turning a manageable problem into an existential crisis. During the Great Depression, the initial financial panic triggered a cascading series of failures that deepened the crisis and made recovery much more difficult. Subversive forces can exploit this panic, using fear and uncertainty to push societies toward more extreme responses.

Radical Responses: The Lure of Extremism

In times of crisis, when traditional solutions seem to have failed, people often turn to radical alternatives. This is fertile ground for extremists of all stripes—political, religious, or ideological—who promise to restore order or provide simple answers to complex problems.

Case Study: The Rise of Fascism in Europe

The rise of fascism in Europe during the 1920s and 1930s is a classic example of how crisis can lead to the embrace of radical ideologies. In the aftermath of World War I, many European countries were in a state of turmoil. Economies were in ruins, political systems were unstable, and social unrest was widespread.

In this environment, extremist parties like the Nazis in Germany and the Fascists in Italy gained traction by promising to restore national pride, economic stability, and social order. They capitalized on public fear and anger, blaming scapegoats—whether it was Jews, Communists, or other perceived enemies—and offering a vision of a strong, authoritarian state that would protect the people.

These movements quickly gained power, often through a combination of democratic processes and violent suppression of opposition. Once in power, they dismantled democratic institutions and imposed totalitarian regimes that led their countries—and much of the world—into the catastrophe of World War II.

Analysis: The Dangers of Extremism in Crisis

The rise of fascism in Europe demonstrates how crises can open the door to radical ideologies that would otherwise have little appeal. In times of uncertainty, people are often willing to sacrifice freedom for the promise of security, making them vulnerable to extremist leaders who exploit their fears. Once these leaders gain power, it can be difficult, if not impossible, to remove them without significant violence and upheaval.

Manufactured Crises: When Crisis is a Strategy

Not all crises are organic. In some cases, subversive elements intentionally create or amplify crises to achieve their goals. By engineering a crisis, they can manipulate the public and push through changes that would be impossible under normal circumstances.

Case Study: The Reichstag Fire

One of the most infamous examples of a manufactured crisis is the Reichstag Fire in 1933, which Adolf Hitler used to consolidate his power in Germany. The Reichstag, the German parliament building, was set on fire in February 1933. The Nazis quickly blamed the fire on Communists, claiming it was the first step in a broader Communist uprising.

In response, Hitler convinced President Hindenburg to sign the Reichstag Fire Decree, which suspended civil liberties and allowed the Nazis to arrest and detain political opponents without trial. This decree, along with the Enabling Act passed shortly afterward, gave Hitler the legal framework he needed to establish a totalitarian regime.

While it's still debated whether the Nazis were directly responsible for the fire, what is clear is that they used the crisis to their advantage, turning a moment of national panic into a stepping stone toward dictatorship.

Analysis: The Power of Manufactured Crises

Manufactured crises are a powerful tool for subversion. By creating or exploiting a crisis, subversive forces can push through radical changes that would never be accepted in normal times. The Reichstag Fire shows how a single, well-timed crisis can be used to dismantle democratic institutions and establish authoritarian control. It's a stark reminder of how fragile democracy can be in the face of manufactured chaos.

Crisis and Opportunity: The Thin Line Between Collapse and Transformation

It's important to recognize that while crises are dangerous, they can also be moments of opportunity. A crisis is a turning point—a moment when things can go either way. While crises often lead to negative outcomes, they can also be a catalyst for positive change, depending on how they are managed.

Case Study: The New Deal in the United States

The Great Depression was a time of immense suffering, but it also led to one of the most significant transformations in American history: the New Deal. Under President Franklin D. Roosevelt, the U.S. government implemented a series of reforms designed to stabilize the economy, provide relief to those suffering, and prevent future crises.

The New Deal included measures like Social Security, unemployment insurance, and the creation of jobs through public works projects. It also introduced regulations to prevent the kinds of financial abuses that had contributed to the Depression. While not without controversy, the New Deal helped to restore public confidence and laid the groundwork for the modern welfare state.

Analysis: Turning Crisis into Opportunity

The New Deal shows that crises don't have to lead to disaster. With strong leadership and a willingness to innovate, it's possible to use a crisis as an opportunity to rebuild and strengthen society. However, this requires a clear vision, effective communication, and the ability to resist the lure of extremist solutions.

Conclusion of Chapter 3:

Crisis is the most dangerous stage of subversion, but it's also the most revealing. It's a moment of truth, where the strengths and weaknesses of a society are laid bare. In a crisis, the choices that leaders and citizens make can determine the fate of the nation—whether it descends into chaos or emerges stronger and more resilient.

The key to surviving a crisis is preparedness. This means not only having strong institutions and effective leadership but also a public that is informed, engaged, and resilient. It's also crucial to recognize the signs of a manufactured crisis and to resist the temptation to embrace radical solutions that promise quick fixes but often lead to disaster.

In the next chapter, we'll explore the final stage of subversion: normalization. We'll see how, after the chaos of crisis, new powers seek to stabilize and consolidate their control, often at the expense of freedom and democracy.

Chapter 4: Normalization - The Final Stage

Normalization is a deceptive term. It suggests a return to order, stability, and routine, but in the context of subversion, it often marks the consolidation of a new order—one that is fundamentally different from what came before. This is the stage where the changes brought about by crisis are solidified, where new power structures take root, and where society is restructured to reflect the interests of those who have seized control during the chaos.

In this chapter, we'll explore how normalization functions as the final stage of subversion, the strategies used to cement the new order, and the long-term consequences for societies that undergo this transformation. We'll also examine historical and contemporary examples to understand how normalization can either entrench authoritarianism or, in rare cases, set the stage for a more just and stable society.

What is Normalization?

Normalization is the process of stabilizing a society after a crisis, but it's important to recognize that what's being stabilized isn't the old order—it's the new one. The changes that occurred during the crisis are cemented, and the society is restructured in ways that reflect the interests and ideologies of those who emerged victorious from the chaos.

The hallmark of normalization is the establishment of new norms and rules that seem to offer security and stability, but often at the cost of freedom, democracy, and diversity. The public, exhausted by the crisis, is often willing to accept these changes in exchange for a sense of normalcy, even if it means sacrificing some of their previous rights and liberties.

Key Aspects of Normalization

1. **Consolidation of Power:** The new ruling class or regime solidifies its control over society, often through legal or extralegal means.
2. **Suppression of Opposition:** Dissenting voices are silenced or marginalized, ensuring that the new order is not challenged.
3. **Rewriting of History:** The narrative of the crisis and its aftermath is controlled and reshaped to legitimize the new power structure.
4. **Institutional Reconfiguration:** Institutions are restructured or replaced to align with the new order, ensuring that the changes are enduring.

Let's delve into how normalization unfolds and what it means for societies that undergo this transformation.

Consolidation of Power: Cementing the New Order

After a crisis, the first priority of those who have gained power is to consolidate their control. This involves not only securing their position but also ensuring that the new order is sustainable over the long term.

Case Study: The Aftermath of the 1968 Prague Spring

The Prague Spring of 1968 was a period of political liberalization in Czechoslovakia, where the Communist government, led by Alexander Dubček, attempted to implement reforms that would grant more freedoms and reduce the influence of the Soviet Union. However, the movement was crushed when Warsaw Pact troops invaded the country in August 1968.

Following the invasion, the Soviet Union imposed a period of "normalization," which involved the reassertion of hardline Communist control. Dubček was replaced, and the reforms were rolled back. The new leadership, under Gustav Husák, purged reformists from the government, media, and educational institutions. The narrative of the Prague Spring was rewritten as a counter-revolutionary attempt that had to be suppressed to protect socialism.

Analysis: How Power is Consolidated in Normalization

The Soviet-led normalization in Czechoslovakia illustrates how a new regime quickly moves to eliminate any remnants of the old order and secure its control. By purging reformists and rewriting the history of the Prague Spring, the new leadership ensured that there would be no further challenges to their authority. This process of consolidation is essential for any new regime seeking to establish long-term stability, even if it comes at the cost of individual freedoms and democratic principles.

Suppression of Opposition: Silencing Dissent

In the normalization phase, opposition is not just discouraged—it's actively suppressed. Those who resist the new order are marginalized, imprisoned, or worse, as the regime seeks to eliminate any potential threats to its authority.

Case Study: The Chinese Cultural Revolution and Its Aftermath

The Cultural Revolution in China (1966–1976) was a period of intense social and political upheaval, orchestrated by Mao Zedong to reinforce his control over the Communist Party and to reassert revolutionary ideology. After Mao's death in 1976, the Chinese government sought to "normalize" the situation by ending the Cultural Revolution's chaos and returning to economic and political stability.

However, this normalization didn't involve a return to the pre-Cultural Revolution order. Instead, the new leadership under Deng Xiaoping suppressed Maoist radicals, including the "Gang of Four," who were blamed for the excesses of the Cultural Revolution. This was followed by economic reforms that opened China to global markets, while political dissent was ruthlessly suppressed, culminating in the Tiananmen Square Massacre in 1989.

Analysis: The Role of Repression in Normalization

The aftermath of the Cultural Revolution shows how normalization can involve a mix of liberalization (in this case, economic) and repression (political). By eliminating radical elements and suppressing dissent, the Chinese government was able to stabilize the country and embark on a path of rapid economic growth. However, this came at the cost of political freedoms, as the government made it clear that any challenge to its authority would not be tolerated.

Rewriting of History: Controlling the Narrative

One of the most effective tools of normalization is the rewriting of history. By controlling the narrative of the crisis and its aftermath, the new regime can legitimize its actions and discredit its opponents.

Case Study: The Russian Narrative on the Annexation of Crimea

In 2014, Russia annexed Crimea from Ukraine, a move that was widely condemned by the international community. However, within Russia, the government presented the annexation as a legitimate "reunification" of historically Russian territory, supported by the will of the Crimean people.

To solidify this narrative, the Russian government launched a comprehensive propaganda campaign, both domestically and internationally. History books were rewritten to emphasize Crimea's Russian identity, and state-controlled media reinforced the narrative that the annexation was a defensive measure against Western encroachment. Dissenting voices, both in Crimea and in Russia, were silenced through censorship and repression.

Analysis: The Power of Historical Revisionism

The rewriting of history is a powerful tool for any regime seeking to normalize its control after a crisis. By controlling the narrative, the regime can shape public perception, justify its actions, and delegitimize its opponents. The Russian government's handling of the Crimea annexation is a clear example of how history can be rewritten to serve the interests of those in power, creating a new "normal" that aligns with the regime's goals.

Institutional Reconfiguration: Reshaping Society

In the normalization phase, institutions that were destabilized or destroyed during the crisis are often reconfigured to align with the new order. This ensures that the changes brought about by the crisis are not just temporary, but become embedded in the fabric of society.

Case Study: Post-War Reconstruction in Eastern Europe

After World War II, the Soviet Union established Communist regimes across Eastern Europe. The process of normalization in these countries involved the complete restructuring of political, economic, and social institutions to align with Soviet-style socialism.

In countries like East Germany, Poland, and Hungary, the Communist Party became the central institution, controlling all aspects of life. Independent institutions, such as religious organizations, labor unions, and political parties, were either co-opted or dismantled. The education system was restructured to promote Marxist-Leninist ideology, and the economy was centralized under state control.

Analysis: The Long-Term Impact of Institutional Reconfiguration

The reconfiguration of institutions during normalization ensures that the changes brought about by the crisis are not easily reversed. By embedding the new order into the very structure of society, the regime makes it difficult for any opposition to arise. The experience of Eastern Europe after World War II demonstrates how effective this strategy can be in creating a stable, albeit authoritarian, system that can endure for decades.

Normalization and Its Consequences: Stability at a Price

While normalization often brings a sense of stability after the chaos of a crisis, it comes at a significant cost. The new order is typically less free, less democratic, and less diverse than what came before. Rights that were lost during the crisis are rarely fully restored, and the society that emerges is often more repressive and less tolerant of dissent.

Case Study: The Islamic Republic of Iran

The 1979 Iranian Revolution led to the overthrow of the Shah and the establishment of an Islamic Republic under Ayatollah Khomeini. The crisis phase of the revolution was marked by widespread violence, political purges, and the establishment of a theocratic regime.

The normalization that followed involved the consolidation of clerical power, the suppression of secular and liberal elements, and the restructuring of Iranian society along the lines of Islamic law. The new regime implemented strict controls over personal behavior, enforced by religious police, and limited political freedoms, creating a highly controlled and authoritarian society.

Analysis: The Price of Stability

The Islamic Republic of Iran is an example of how normalization can create a stable but repressive society. While the regime succeeded in consolidating its power and maintaining order, it did so at the expense of political freedoms, personal liberties, and cultural diversity. This trade-off is common in many cases of normalization, where the desire for stability leads to the acceptance of authoritarianism.

Conclusion of Chapter 4:

Normalization is the final stage of subversion, but it's far from a return to the old order. Instead, it's about consolidating the new power structures that emerged during the crisis, suppressing opposition, and reshaping society to ensure that the changes are permanent. While normalization can bring stability, it often does so at the cost of freedom, democracy, and diversity.

The key to resisting the negative aspects of normalization lies in vigilance. It requires a commitment to preserving democratic institutions, protecting individual rights, and challenging the rewriting of history. Without these efforts, normalization can lead to the entrenchment of authoritarianism, creating a society that is stable but not free.

In the next part of the book, we'll shift our focus to contemporary examples of subversion and explore how these processes are playing out in the modern world. We'll look at how subversive tactics are being used today, the new technologies that are amplifying their impact, and what can be done to resist these threats in the 21st century.

The manipulation of identity politics is a tactic that has been used by various global powers, including Western nations, to achieve their strategic goals. The challenge for democracies is to manage identity-based issues in a way that promotes unity and inclusion, rather than division and conflict.

Chapter 5: The Subversion of Western Democracies

Western democracies, long considered robust and resilient, have faced growing challenges from both foreign and domestic subversive activities. The 21st century has seen the rise of new tactics, particularly in the digital realm, that exploit the openness and pluralism of democratic societies. While foreign powers such as Russia and China are often highlighted in discussions of subversion, it's essential to recognize that domestic actors can—and do—play significant roles in these processes as well.

This chapter explores the role of social media in the 2016 U.S. presidential election, the rise of identity politics, and the broader implications of both domestic and foreign subversion in Western democracies.

The Role of Social Media: A Tool for Domestic Subversion

Social media platforms have revolutionized global communication, creating spaces for public discourse and political mobilization. However, these platforms have also become tools for subversion, where the line between foreign and domestic influence is often blurred. The 2016 U.S. presidential election is a prime example of how social media can be used for subversive purposes, not just by foreign entities, but by domestic actors as well.

Case Study: The 2016 U.S. Presidential Election

In the aftermath of the 2016 election, widespread claims emerged that Russia had used social media to interfere with the election process, primarily through disinformation campaigns and the use of bots. However, subsequent investigations, including revelations from the Twitter Files and statements by Mark Zuckerberg of Facebook, have complicated this narrative. These sources suggest that U.S. intelligence agencies, particularly the FBI, may have played a significant role in shaping the flow of information on these platforms, feeding misinformation that contributed to public perceptions of foreign interference.

This situation illustrates a complex form of domestic subversion, where internal institutions and actors may have influenced the election process under the guise of countering foreign threats. The result was a highly polarized political environment where trust in both media and government institutions was significantly eroded.

Analysis: The Intersection of Domestic and Foreign Subversion

The 2016 election highlighted the challenges of distinguishing between foreign and domestic subversion in the digital age. While the initial focus was on Russia's potential influence, it became clear that domestic actors also played a crucial role in shaping the narrative and public perception. The involvement of U.S. intelligence agencies in monitoring and influencing social media content raises important questions about the integrity of democratic processes and the balance of power between state institutions and the public.

This case underscores the need for greater transparency and accountability in how information is managed and disseminated, both by social media platforms and government agencies. It also illustrates how domestic subversion can be as destabilizing as foreign interference, particularly when it undermines public trust in democratic institutions.

The Crisis of Identity Politics: Fragmenting Societies

Identity politics—the focus on the interests of specific social groups based on characteristics like race, gender, sexuality, or religion—has become a central feature of political discourse in many Western democracies. While it can be a powerful force for social justice and advocacy, identity politics can also be exploited to create divisions and weaken national unity.

Case Study: The Fragmentation of Political Discourse in the United States

In recent years, identity politics has become a significant factor in the political landscape of the United States. Movements like Black Lives Matter and #MeToo have brought important issues of racial and gender inequality to the forefront, demanding systemic change. On the other side of the spectrum, movements like the alt-right have utilized identity politics to promote nationalism and white supremacy.

Social media and partisan media outlets have amplified these movements, creating echo chambers where individuals are primarily exposed to information that reinforces their existing beliefs. This has led to a fragmentation of political discourse, where finding common ground has become increasingly difficult.

However, it's crucial to recognize that identity politics and its exploitation are not phenomena limited to any one region or political ideology. Western powers have historically used identity-based divisions as tools in foreign policy, supporting groups that align with their strategic interests while undermining those that do not.

Analysis: The Dangers of a Fragmented Society

While identity politics can drive necessary social change, it can also be manipulated to fragment societies. When political discourse centers around identity, it becomes easier to pit groups against one another, fostering an "us versus them" mentality. This division can be exploited by both foreign and domestic actors to weaken democratic institutions and erode social cohesion.

The manipulation of identity politics is a tactic that has been used by various global powers, including Western nations, to achieve their strategic goals. The challenge for democracies is to manage identity-based issues in a way that promotes unity and inclusion, rather than division and conflict.

Foreign Influence: A Global Game of Subversion

The influence of foreign actors in domestic politics is an age-old strategy, but the methods and scale of such influence have transformed dramatically in the digital age. State and non-state actors now use the internet to interfere in the political processes of other countries with unprecedented sophistication and reach.

Case Study: Global Subversion and the New Cold War

Beyond the United States, Russia and China have been implicated in efforts to influence elections and political discourse in several Western countries. In France's 2017 presidential election, Russian hackers leaked emails from Emmanuel Macron's campaign in an attempt to sway public opinion. In the United Kingdom, Russian-funded media outlets like RT and Sputnik have been accused of spreading disinformation related to Brexit.

Yet, it's important to acknowledge that the West has also engaged in similar practices. Throughout the Cold War and beyond, Western nations have used various tools—ranging from public broadcasting to economic pressures exerted by institutions like the International Monetary Fund (IMF)—to influence political outcomes in other countries. These efforts, while often presented as promoting democracy and stability, have sometimes led to unintended consequences, including long-term resentment and regional destabilization.

Analysis: The Global Impact of Foreign Subversion

Subversion in the information age is a global issue, with no single nation or bloc holding a monopoly on these tactics. As countries like Russia and China develop more sophisticated means of influencing foreign electorates, Western democracies must also reflect on their own history of influence and subversion. Addressing these challenges requires a multifaceted approach—improving cybersecurity, regulating social media, and, crucially, fostering public awareness and resilience against all forms of disinformation, regardless of their origin.

In a globalized world, where information and influence cross borders with ease, the task of protecting democratic processes is more complex than ever. Nations must be vigilant not only against foreign subversion but also against the ways in which their own actions can contribute to instability elsewhere.

Conclusion of Chapter 5:

The subversion of Western democracies is part of a larger, global phenomenon where multiple actors—both state and non-state, foreign and domestic—use a variety of tools to influence political outcomes. Social media, identity politics, and foreign influence campaigns are powerful instruments in this new era of subversion, but they are wielded by many hands, each with its own agenda.

The 2016 U.S. presidential election serves as a key example of how domestic subversion can be as impactful as foreign interference, with significant implications for public trust and the integrity of democratic processes. Moving forward, it is crucial for democracies to strengthen their institutions, promote transparency, and foster unity in the face of both domestic and foreign threats.

In the next chapter, we'll explore the concept of the "new cold war" and how subversion is being carried out by major global powers in the age of information. We'll examine the tactics used by countries like Russia, China, and Western nations to extend their influence and the implications for global security.

Chapter 6: The New Cold War - Subversion in the Age of Information

The modern world is witnessing a new form of global competition—one that is less about direct military confrontation and more about information, influence, and subversion. This "new cold war" is being fought not with tanks and missiles, but through cyberattacks, media manipulation, economic leverage, and strategic influence operations. While many of the tactics are familiar, dating back to the geopolitical struggles of the 20th century, the tools of subversion have evolved significantly in the digital age, making these methods more potent and pervasive than ever before.

In this chapter, we'll explore how subversion is being deployed by major global powers—Russia, China, and Western nations—within the context of this new cold war. We'll look at how these nations use disinformation, economic pressure, and cyber operations to extend their influence, weaken rivals, and shape global outcomes. Finally, we'll consider the implications of these strategies for global security, political stability, and the future of international relations.

Russia's Playbook: Hybrid Warfare and Strategic Influence

Russia has been one of the most prominent players in the new cold war, using a strategy commonly referred to as "hybrid warfare." This approach blends conventional military tactics with non-military tools, such as cyberattacks, disinformation campaigns, economic coercion, and political subversion, to destabilize rivals and achieve geopolitical objectives.

Case Study: The Annexation of Crimea

The 2014 annexation of Crimea by Russia is a complex and multifaceted event, deeply rooted in the region's history, geopolitics, and ethnic tensions. Crimea, a region with a significant Russian-speaking population, has long held strategic importance for Russia due to its location and the presence of the Black Sea Fleet in Sevastopol.

The situation in Crimea escalated in the context of the broader Ukraine crisis, which began with mass protests in Kyiv (known as the Euromaidan) that led to the ousting of Ukraine's then-President Viktor Yanukovych in February 2014. The new Ukrainian government was seen by Moscow as Western-leaning and potentially aligned with NATO, posing a significant strategic threat to Russia, particularly given NATO's eastward expansion over the previous decades.

Amid the political upheaval, tensions rose in the ethnically Russian regions of Ukraine, particularly in Crimea and the Donbass. In the Donbass, a conflict erupted between Ukrainian forces and pro-Russian separatists, leading to significant casualties on both sides. Reports of persecution and violence against ethnic Russians in these regions fueled fears in Crimea, where many residents viewed the new Ukrainian government with suspicion and concern.

In response to the unfolding crisis, Russia moved quickly to secure its interests in Crimea. Unmarked Russian soldiers—often referred to as "little green men"—took control of key facilities across the peninsula. Meanwhile, a controversial referendum was organized in Crimea, with the result overwhelmingly in favor of joining Russia. While the referendum was widely criticized by the international community as illegitimate, Russia swiftly annexed Crimea, citing the need to protect ethnic Russians and its strategic interests.

Analysis: The Complex Dynamics of Crimea's Annexation

The annexation of Crimea by Russia is often portrayed differently depending on the perspective. From Russia's viewpoint, the move was a defensive action aimed at protecting its strategic interests and the rights of ethnic Russians in the face of what it perceived as an encroaching NATO and a hostile new government in Ukraine. The annexation was justified by Moscow as a response to the legitimate fears of Crimea's Russian-speaking population, who were reportedly facing increasing hostility in a rapidly changing political landscape.

From the perspective of Ukraine and much of the international community, the annexation is seen as a violation of Ukraine's sovereignty and territorial integrity. The referendum is widely regarded as having been conducted under duress, with the presence of Russian military forces influencing the outcome. Moreover, the annexation is viewed as a destabilizing act that violated international law and set a dangerous precedent for the use of force to alter national borders.

The annexation also highlights the use of hybrid warfare by Russia—combining military presence with political maneuvering and information campaigns. Russian state-controlled media played a crucial role in shaping public perception both within Crimea and in Russia, presenting the annexation as a necessary and justified action. Meanwhile, cyber operations and information warfare were used to disrupt Ukrainian government communications and control the narrative surrounding the events.

This case underscores the complexity of modern subversion, where actions can be interpreted in various ways depending on historical, cultural, and geopolitical contexts. It also illustrates how subversive tactics, such as disinformation and hybrid warfare, can be used to achieve strategic objectives without engaging in full-scale conventional warfare.

China's Silent Influence: Economic Power and Strategic Subversion

While Russia's approach to subversion often involves overt disinformation and military posturing, China's tactics are more subtle, relying heavily on economic influence and soft power. China's strategy focuses on using its growing economic might to gain leverage over other nations, particularly through its ambitious Belt and Road Initiative (BRI) and its increasing investments in strategic industries worldwide.

Case Study: The Belt and Road Initiative (BRI)

The Belt and Road Initiative, launched in 2013, is China's flagship economic development project, aimed at building infrastructure and boosting trade across Asia, Africa, and Europe. Through the BRI, China has invested billions of dollars in building railways, ports, highways, and energy projects, often in countries that are in desperate need of infrastructure improvements.

While the BRI is marketed as a mutually beneficial economic initiative, critics argue that it is a tool of Chinese subversion, designed to entangle developing nations in a web of economic dependency. Many countries that have accepted Chinese loans and investments have found themselves struggling to repay these debts, leading to accusations of "debt-trap diplomacy." In several cases, China has been able to gain control over critical infrastructure projects—such as ports in Sri Lanka and Pakistan—when host countries have defaulted on their loans.

Additionally, China has used the BRI as a platform to export its political influence. Through strategic investments, China can pressure recipient countries to align with its geopolitical interests, including support for its territorial claims in the South China Sea and its stance on Taiwan.

Analysis: Economic Subversion Through the BRI

China's use of the BRI as a tool of subversion is a masterclass in leveraging economic power for political gain. By providing much-needed infrastructure funding to developing nations, China is able to expand its influence across the globe, often in regions where Western influence is waning. However, this economic support often comes with strings attached, as recipient nations find themselves increasingly dependent on China for both financial support and political stability.

Unlike Russia's more overt forms of subversion, China's strategy is subtler and less likely to provoke immediate backlash. Yet, the long-term effects of economic dependency on China could be just as destabilizing, particularly if countries find themselves forced to choose between economic survival and political sovereignty.

The West's Role: A Complex History of Influence Operations

While much of the focus on subversion in the new cold war has been on the actions of Russia and China, it is important to acknowledge that Western nations—especially the United States—have a long history of engaging in subversion themselves. From public diplomacy campaigns to covert operations, the West has used various means to influence political outcomes in other countries, often in the name of promoting democracy or protecting national security.

Case Study: U.S. Influence in Latin America

Throughout the 20th century, the United States engaged in numerous influence operations in Latin America, aimed at preventing the spread of communism and securing its strategic interests in the region. This often involved supporting military coups, funding opposition movements, and using economic pressure to ensure that governments aligned with U.S. interests.

One of the most notorious examples is the 1954 coup in Guatemala, where the CIA orchestrated the overthrow of democratically elected President Jacobo Árbenz. Árbenz's land reform policies threatened the interests of U.S. corporations, particularly the United Fruit Company, and he was perceived as too sympathetic to communism. The coup, while successful in removing Árbenz, led to decades of political instability and civil war in Guatemala.

More recently, the West has used economic sanctions and diplomatic pressure as tools of subversion. Sanctions against countries like Iran, Venezuela, and Russia have been employed to isolate these nations economically and politically, with the aim of either forcing regime change or compelling changes in policy.

Analysis: The Ethical Dilemmas of Western Subversion

Western influence operations, particularly those carried out during the Cold War, raise important ethical questions about the balance between promoting democracy and respecting national sovereignty. While these efforts are often justified as necessary to counter authoritarianism or protect security interests, they have also led to unintended consequences, including the destabilization of regions and the rise of anti-Western sentiment.

In the context of the new cold war, Western nations must be mindful of their own history of influence operations as they seek to counter the subversive actions of rivals like Russia and China. This requires a commitment to transparency, accountability, and genuine respect for the sovereignty of other nations, rather than merely advancing geopolitical interests.

The Role of Cyber Warfare: A New Battlefield

One of the defining features of the new cold war is the centrality of cyberspace as a battleground for subversion. Cyberattacks, disinformation campaigns, and hacking have become common tools for nations seeking to destabilize their rivals, steal valuable information, or gain political leverage.

Case Study: Cyber Attacks on Critical Infrastructure

Over the past decade, cyberattacks targeting critical infrastructure have become a major concern for governments worldwide. In 2020, a major cyberattack attributed to Russia's intelligence agency, known as the SolarWinds hack, breached numerous U.S. government agencies, including the Departments of Homeland Security, State, and Treasury. The attackers were able to access sensitive information for months before the breach was discovered.

Such cyberattacks demonstrate the vulnerability of even the most secure systems and raise serious concerns about the potential for cyber warfare to disrupt essential services, steal valuable intelligence, and even trigger larger military conflicts.

In addition to Russia, China has been implicated in a number of high-profile cyberattacks, particularly those aimed at stealing intellectual property and sensitive government data. These attacks often target industries that are critical to national security, such as defense contractors, energy companies, and pharmaceutical firms.

Analysis: The Growing Threat of Cyber Subversion

As the world becomes increasingly digital, cyber warfare has emerged as one of the most dangerous tools of subversion. Unlike conventional warfare, cyberattacks are difficult to detect, attribute, and defend against, making them an ideal weapon for state and non-state actors alike.

In the context of the new cold war, cyberattacks allow nations to inflict significant damage on their rivals without crossing the traditional threshold of armed conflict. This creates a gray zone where subversion can take place without triggering the kinds of military responses that might arise from more overt forms of aggression.

Conclusion of Chapter 6:

The new cold war is not a conflict defined by military standoffs or territorial conquests, but by the struggle for influence through subversion, cyber warfare, and economic manipulation. Russia's hybrid warfare, China's strategic use of economic leverage, and the legacy of Western influence operations all illustrate the diverse and evolving tactics used by major powers to achieve their geopolitical goals.

As these tactics become more sophisticated, the risks to global security grow. The challenge for the international community is to develop strategies that can effectively counter these subversive actions while promoting stability, transparency, and respect for national sovereignty.

In the next chapter, we'll explore the future of subversion, focusing on emerging threats such as artificial intelligence and the weaponization of globalization. We'll examine how these new tools could redefine subversion in the 21st century and discuss the implications for global peace and security.

Chapter 7: The Future of Subversion - Emerging Threats in the 21st Century

As we move deeper into the 21st century, the tools and tactics of subversion are evolving at a rapid pace. New technologies, global interconnectedness, and the increasing complexity of international relations are giving rise to novel forms of subversion that are more difficult to detect and counter. From artificial intelligence to the weaponization of global supply chains, these emerging threats have the potential to reshape the landscape of global security and challenge the stability of nations in unprecedented ways.

In this chapter, we'll explore the future of subversion by examining these emerging threats. We'll look at how artificial intelligence (AI) is being used to enhance disinformation campaigns, how globalization can be weaponized to exert economic and political pressure, and how the increasing interdependence of global systems is creating new vulnerabilities. Finally, we'll discuss what these developments mean for the future of international relations and how nations can prepare to defend themselves against these new forms of subversion.

Artificial Intelligence and Disinformation: The Next Frontier

Artificial intelligence is revolutionizing many aspects of our lives, from healthcare to finance to entertainment. But AI is also becoming a powerful tool for subversion, particularly in the realm of disinformation. As AI technology becomes more advanced, it enables the creation of more sophisticated and convincing disinformation campaigns that can be deployed on a massive scale.

Case Study: Deepfakes and AI-Driven Disinformation

One of the most concerning developments in AI is the rise of deepfakes—hyper-realistic video and audio forgeries that can make it appear as though someone is saying or doing something they never did. Deepfakes are created using AI algorithms that analyze vast amounts of real video and audio footage to generate highly convincing forgeries. These fakes can be used to create misleading news stories, manipulate public opinion, or discredit political figures.

For example, imagine a deepfake video showing a world leader making inflammatory or irresponsible statements. Such a video could go viral on social media before it's debunked, leading to widespread panic, diplomatic crises, or even conflict. The ability to produce and distribute deepfakes quickly and anonymously makes them a potent tool for subversive actors looking to disrupt political processes or undermine trust in institutions.

In addition to deepfakes, AI-driven disinformation campaigns can use machine learning algorithms to generate and amplify false narratives. Bots powered by AI can flood social media with misleading information, targeting specific demographics with tailored messages designed to sow discord or manipulate opinions.

Analysis: The Challenges of Countering AI-Driven Subversion

The use of AI in disinformation presents significant challenges for governments and societies. The speed and scale at which AI-generated content can be produced and disseminated make it difficult for traditional fact-checking and media organizations to keep up. Moreover, as AI-generated content becomes more sophisticated, it becomes harder for the average person to distinguish between real and fake information.

To counter these threats, new approaches are needed. This includes the development of AI tools that can detect and flag deepfakes and other forms of AI-generated disinformation in real-time. Governments and tech companies must also collaborate to establish standards and regulations for the responsible use of AI, ensuring that this powerful technology is not misused for subversive purposes.

Public awareness and education are equally important. As AI-driven disinformation becomes more prevalent, individuals need to be equipped with the skills to critically evaluate the information they encounter online. This means promoting digital literacy, encouraging skepticism of too-good-to-be-true content, and fostering a culture of verification and trustworthiness in media consumption.

Weaponization of Globalization: Economic Leverage and Strategic Dependency

Globalization has brought about unprecedented levels of economic interdependence, with goods, services, and capital flowing across borders more freely than ever before. While this interconnectedness has driven economic growth and innovation, it has also created new vulnerabilities that can be exploited for subversive purposes. Nations are increasingly using their control over critical resources, supply chains, and financial systems as tools of geopolitical leverage.

Case Study: The Semiconductor Supply Chain Crisis

One of the most striking examples of the weaponization of globalization is the ongoing semiconductor supply chain crisis. Semiconductors, which are essential components in everything from smartphones to military hardware, are produced by a small number of companies in a few countries, notably Taiwan, South Korea, and the United States. The global semiconductor supply chain is highly specialized and concentrated, making it vulnerable to disruption.

In recent years, geopolitical tensions, particularly between the United States and China, have led to increased scrutiny of the semiconductor industry. The U.S. has imposed export controls on semiconductor technology to China, citing national security concerns. In response, China has accelerated its efforts to develop a self-sufficient semiconductor industry, while also exploring ways to leverage its own dominance in other critical industries, such as rare earth minerals, to exert pressure on the West.

The semiconductor shortage, exacerbated by the COVID-19 pandemic, has highlighted the risks of over-reliance on a few key suppliers. It has also underscored how economic interdependence can be weaponized, with countries using control over critical supply chains as a means of exerting geopolitical influence and achieving strategic objectives.

Analysis: The Implications of Economic Subversion

The semiconductor supply chain crisis illustrates how economic subversion can be used as a tool of statecraft in the 21st century. By leveraging control over critical industries and resources, nations can exert significant pressure on their rivals, disrupting economies and forcing political concessions. This form of subversion is particularly effective in a globalized world, where economies are deeply interconnected and reliant on complex supply chains.

To mitigate the risks of economic subversion, nations need to diversify their supply chains, invest in domestic production capabilities, and build strategic reserves of critical resources. International cooperation is also essential to ensure that supply chains are resilient and that no single nation can monopolize control over vital industries.

The Interconnectedness of Global Systems: New Vulnerabilities and Opportunities

As the world becomes more interconnected, the potential for both subversion and cooperation increases. Global systems—ranging from financial networks to communication infrastructure to public health initiatives—are now so intertwined that disruptions in one area can have cascading effects across the globe. This interconnectedness presents both new vulnerabilities and new opportunities for subversive actors.

Case Study: The COVID-19 Pandemic

The COVID-19 pandemic has been a stark reminder of the vulnerabilities inherent in a highly interconnected world. The rapid spread of the virus across borders, the global shortages of medical supplies, and the economic disruptions caused by lockdowns have all demonstrated how interconnected global systems are and how easily they can be disrupted.

While the pandemic itself is a natural phenomenon, the response to it has highlighted the potential for subversive actions. Disinformation about the virus, its origins, and the effectiveness of vaccines has spread rapidly online, often fueled by both state and non-state actors seeking to exploit the crisis for political or financial gain. Meanwhile, the competition for medical supplies and vaccines has led to accusations of "vaccine nationalism," where countries prioritize their own populations at the expense of global cooperation.

The pandemic has also exposed the risks of over-reliance on global supply chains, particularly in critical sectors like healthcare. The shortages of personal protective equipment (PPE) and other medical supplies early in the pandemic were exacerbated by the fact that much of the production capacity for these items is concentrated in a few countries.

Analysis: Navigating a Hyper-Connected World

The COVID-19 pandemic underscores the need for resilience in a hyper-connected world. As global systems become more integrated, the potential for cascading failures and subversive actions increases. Nations must prioritize building resilient infrastructure, diversifying supply chains, and fostering international cooperation to navigate these challenges.

At the same time, the interconnectedness of global systems also presents opportunities for positive subversion—using global networks to promote peace, stability, and shared prosperity. By leveraging these connections for constructive purposes, nations can counteract the negative aspects of subversion and build a more secure and cooperative global order.

Conclusion of Chapter 7:

The future of subversion is shaped by the emerging threats and opportunities of the 21st century. Artificial intelligence, the weaponization of globalization, and the interconnectedness of global systems are all transforming the landscape of subversion, creating new challenges for nations and international organizations.

As these threats evolve, so too must the strategies for countering them. This will require innovation, collaboration, and a commitment to building resilient systems that can withstand the pressures of subversion. By understanding the tools and tactics of modern subversion, nations can better prepare to defend themselves and promote a more stable and secure global order.

In the final part of the book, we'll explore strategies for resilience and counter-subversion, discussing how nations can protect themselves from these emerging threats while fostering a global environment that prioritizes peace, cooperation, and mutual respect.

Resilience and Counter-Subversion - Strategies for a Secure Future

Having explored the various forms of subversion and the emerging threats that challenge global security in the 21st century, it's now essential to focus on how nations can protect themselves. Building resilience and developing effective counter-subversion strategies are critical to safeguarding democratic institutions, economic stability, and social cohesion.

In this final part of the book, we'll discuss practical approaches to countering subversion. We'll explore strategies for strengthening democratic resilience, fostering global cooperation, and utilizing technology responsibly. We'll also look at how education, media literacy, and transparency can play a pivotal role in empowering individuals and communities to resist subversive influences. Finally, we'll consider how a commitment to ethical governance and respect for international norms can help create a global environment less conducive to subversive tactics.

Chapter 8: Strengthening Democratic Resilience

Democracies, with their inherent openness and pluralism, are particularly vulnerable to subversion. However, they also possess unique strengths that can be harnessed to build resilience against these threats. In this chapter, we'll explore how democratic institutions can be fortified, how civic engagement can be encouraged, and how transparency and accountability can be maintained to protect against subversion.

Fortifying Democratic Institutions

At the heart of any democracy are its institutions—government bodies, courts, electoral systems, and the media. These institutions are often the primary targets of subversive activities, as weakening them can destabilize the entire society. To build resilience, it's essential to strengthen these institutions against both internal and external threats.

Protecting Electoral Integrity

Elections are a cornerstone of democracy, and ensuring their integrity is crucial for maintaining public trust. This includes protecting against both foreign interference and domestic manipulation. Strategies to enhance electoral resilience include:

- **Securing Election Infrastructure:** Investing in cybersecurity to protect voting systems from hacking and ensuring that election results are accurate and tamper-proof.
- **Promoting Transparency:** Ensuring that election processes are transparent and that any allegations of irregularities are investigated swiftly and openly.
- **Combating Disinformation:** Implementing measures to identify and counter disinformation campaigns that seek to influence voter behavior or undermine confidence in the electoral process.

Strengthening the Rule of Law

The rule of law is essential for the functioning of democracy, ensuring that laws are applied consistently and fairly. To protect against subversion, it's important to reinforce the independence of the judiciary and maintain a legal framework that resists corruption and political interference. Key strategies include:

- **Judicial Independence:** Safeguarding the judiciary from political pressure and ensuring that judges can make decisions based on law and evidence, not external influence.
- **Anti-Corruption Measures:** Strengthening anti-corruption laws and institutions to prevent the abuse of power and ensure that public officials are held accountable for their actions.

Encouraging Civic Engagement

A vibrant civil society is one of the strongest defenses against subversion. When citizens are actively engaged in their communities and participate in the political process, it becomes much harder for subversive actors to manipulate public opinion or undermine democratic norms.

Encouraging civic engagement involves:

- **Promoting Education and Media Literacy:** Equipping citizens with the knowledge and skills to critically evaluate information, recognize disinformation, and engage in informed decision-making.
- **Supporting Civil Society Organizations:** Ensuring that non-governmental organizations (NGOs) and community groups have the resources and freedom to operate independently, advocate for citizens' rights, and hold governments accountable.
- **Facilitating Open Dialogue:** Creating platforms for open and respectful dialogue among citizens, enabling diverse voices to be heard and fostering a sense of shared community and common purpose.

Maintaining Transparency and Accountability

Transparency and accountability are essential for preventing subversion from within. When governments operate transparently and officials are held accountable for their actions, it reduces the opportunities for subversive elements to exploit weaknesses in the system.

- **Open Government Initiatives:** Promoting policies that ensure government actions and decisions are transparent, including open access to information and public oversight mechanisms.
- **Whistleblower Protections:** Encouraging and protecting whistleblowers who expose corruption, fraud, or other forms of misconduct, ensuring they can come forward without fear of retaliation.
- **Independent Media:** Supporting a free and independent press that can investigate and report on government actions, providing a check on power and exposing any subversive activities.

Chapter 9: Fostering Global Cooperation

In an increasingly interconnected world, no country can address the challenges of subversion alone. Global cooperation is essential for countering transnational threats, from cyberattacks to disinformation campaigns. In this chapter, we'll explore how international collaboration can strengthen global security, promote shared norms, and build collective resilience against subversive actions.

Building Cybersecurity Alliances

As cyber threats become more sophisticated and pervasive, international cooperation on cybersecurity is crucial. Countries must work together to share intelligence, develop common standards, and respond to cyberattacks in a coordinated manner.

Case Study: The European Union's Cybersecurity Strategy

The European Union (EU) has made significant strides in developing a comprehensive cybersecurity strategy that emphasizes cooperation among member states. This includes the creation of the European Union Agency for Cybersecurity (ENISA), which coordinates efforts to improve cybersecurity across the EU, provides support to member states, and promotes the adoption of best practices.

The EU's approach to cybersecurity highlights the importance of collective action in addressing cyber threats. By pooling resources and expertise, EU member states are better equipped to defend against cyberattacks and respond quickly when incidents occur.

Promoting International Cyber Norms

Establishing international norms for behavior in cyberspace is another critical aspect of global cooperation. By agreeing on what constitutes acceptable conduct in cyberspace—and what doesn't—countries can reduce the risk of conflict and build trust.

Key steps include:

- **Developing International Agreements:** Building on existing frameworks like the United Nations Group of Governmental Experts (UN GGE) on cybersecurity to create binding international agreements that define and enforce norms of responsible state behavior in cyberspace.
- **Enhancing Cross-Border Cooperation:** Facilitating information sharing and joint operations among national cybersecurity agencies to address cross-border cyber threats more effectively.

Strengthening Multilateral Institutions

Multilateral institutions play a vital role in addressing global challenges, from economic instability to conflict resolution. Strengthening these institutions and ensuring they are equipped to handle the complexities of modern subversion is crucial for maintaining global security.

Revitalizing the United Nations

The United Nations (UN) remains a central platform for international cooperation, but it must adapt to address the emerging challenges of the 21st century. This includes:

- **Enhancing the UN's Role in Cybersecurity:** Expanding the

UN's capacity to address cyber threats, including through the establishment of a dedicated body to coordinate international efforts on cybersecurity.

- **Supporting Conflict Prevention and Resolution:** Strengthening the UN's ability to prevent and resolve conflicts that arise from subversive actions, including through enhanced mediation and peacekeeping capabilities.
- **Promoting Inclusive Global Governance:** Ensuring that all nations, regardless of size or power, have a voice in global decision-making processes, thereby fostering a sense of shared responsibility and mutual respect.

Regional Cooperation

In addition to global institutions, regional organizations play a crucial role in building resilience against subversion. By fostering cooperation among neighboring countries, these organizations can address regional challenges more effectively.

- **Case Study: The African Union's Role in Conflict Resolution**

The African Union (AU) has increasingly taken on a leadership role in resolving conflicts and promoting peace across the continent. Through initiatives like the African Peace and Security Architecture (APSA), the AU works to prevent conflicts, mediate disputes, and promote stability in member states. This regional approach to conflict resolution highlights the importance of localized efforts to counter subversion and build resilience.

Chapter 10: The Role of Technology and Innovation

Technology is a double-edged sword in the fight against subversion. While it can be used to spread disinformation and disrupt societies, it also offers powerful tools for detecting and countering subversive activities. In this chapter, we'll explore how technology and innovation can be harnessed to protect against subversion and strengthen democratic institutions.

Harnessing Artificial Intelligence for Good

Artificial intelligence (AI) has the potential to be a powerful ally in the fight against subversion. By developing AI tools that can detect disinformation, identify cyber threats, and protect critical infrastructure, nations can enhance their ability to respond to emerging challenges.

Developing AI for Disinformation Detection

AI can be used to detect and combat disinformation by analyzing large volumes of online content, identifying patterns, and flagging potentially misleading information. This includes:

- **Natural Language Processing (NLP):** Using AI-driven NLP tools to analyze text and identify disinformation based on tone, sentiment, and content patterns.
- **Image and Video Analysis:** Deploying AI to analyze visual content, such as deepfakes, and determine its authenticity.
- **Real-Time Monitoring:** Leveraging AI to monitor social media platforms in real-time, identifying and mitigating the spread of disinformation before it gains traction.

Protecting Critical Infrastructure with AI

AI can also play a key role in protecting critical infrastructure from cyberattacks. By analyzing network traffic, identifying anomalies, and predicting potential threats, AI-driven cybersecurity systems can enhance the resilience of essential services, such as energy grids, transportation systems, and financial networks.

Balancing Innovation with Ethics

As technology continues to evolve, it's essential to balance innovation with ethical considerations. This includes ensuring that AI and other technologies are developed and used in ways that respect privacy, protect human rights, and promote transparency.

- **Ethical AI Development:** Establishing guidelines and frameworks for the ethical development and use of AI, including ensuring that AI systems are transparent, explainable, and accountable.
- **Public Engagement:** Involving the public in discussions about the ethical implications of new technologies, ensuring that societal values are reflected in how these technologies are developed and deployed.

Chapter 11: Education, Media Literacy, and Public Awareness

Empowering citizens to resist subversion is a critical component of building national resilience. This requires a focus on education, media literacy, and public awareness, ensuring that individuals are equipped with the knowledge and skills to navigate an increasingly complex information landscape.

Promoting Media Literacy

Media literacy is essential for helping individuals critically evaluate the information they encounter and recognize disinformation. This involves:

- **Integrating Media Literacy into Education:** Incorporating media literacy education into school curricula, teaching students how to critically assess sources, verify information, and understand the impact of media on society.
- **Public Awareness Campaigns:** Launching public awareness campaigns to educate citizens about the dangers of disinformation and the importance of critical thinking.
- **Supporting Independent Media:** Encouraging the development of independent media outlets that provide accurate, unbiased

information and serve as a counterbalance to disinformation.

Fostering a Culture of Critical Thinking

Critical thinking is the foundation of resilience against subversion. By fostering a culture that values inquiry, skepticism, and evidence-based decision-making, societies can become more resistant to manipulation and subversive tactics.

- **Encouraging Open Dialogue:** Promoting open and respectful dialogue on contentious issues, allowing individuals to express diverse viewpoints and engage in constructive debate.
- **Teaching Problem-Solving Skills:** Incorporating problem-solving and analytical skills into education at all levels, helping individuals think critically about complex issues and make informed decisions.

Building Trust Through Transparency

Trust is a key component of resilience. When citizens trust their institutions, they are less susceptible to subversion. Building trust requires transparency in government actions, open communication, and accountability.

- **Open Government Practices:** Implementing policies that ensure government actions and decisions are transparent, including public access to information and regular communication with citizens.
- **Engaging with Communities:** Involving communities in decision-making processes, ensuring that citizens feel heard and valued, and fostering a sense of shared responsibility for the well-being of society.

Conclusion: A Blueprint for Resilience

The challenges of subversion in the 21st century are complex and multifaceted, but they are not insurmountable. By strengthening democratic institutions, fostering global cooperation, harnessing technology responsibly, and empowering citizens through education and media literacy, nations can build resilience against these emerging threats.

The path forward requires a commitment to transparency, accountability, and ethical governance, both at the national and international levels. It also demands a recognition that the fight against subversion is not just the responsibility of governments, but of all citizens who value freedom, democracy, and peace.

As we move into an increasingly interconnected and technologically advanced world, the strategies outlined in this book offer a blueprint for building a more secure and resilient global order. By working together, we can create a future where subversion is met not with fear or complacency, but with strength, unity, and unwavering commitment to the principles that underpin our societies.